Getting to know Saint
Jeanne Jugan
Foundress of the Little Sisters of the Poor

Didier Chardez

coccinelle
éditions

© Didier Chardez - Coccinelle BD asbl
5, Allée Louis de Loncin, B-6940 Durbuy

Les Petites Sœurs des Pauvres
Maison-Mère
La Tour Saint-Joseph F-35190 ST PERN

Original title : « À la rencontre de Sainte JEANNE JUGAN, Fondatrice des Petites Sœurs des Pauvres »
Translation : Little Sisters of the Poor

D/2013/8475/72
ISBN 978-2-930273-72-3

bd@coccinelle-editions.be
www.coccinelle-editions.be

THE NEXT DAY, EARLY IN THE MORNING...

HERE WE ARE IN CANCALE! THIS IS WHERE JEANNE JUGAN WAS BORN OCTOBER 25, 1792...

WAAAAAAAAH!

IT'S A LITTLE GIRL!

YOU CAN COME IN, CHILDREN! COME GIVE YOUR LITTLE SISTER A KISS!

SHE'S ALL RED! SHE'S FUNNY!

IT'S TOO BAD DAD IS AWAY AT SEA.

YES, IT'S A SHAME, MARIE JOSEPH; BY THE TIME DAD SEES HER SHE'LL BE ALMOST A MONTH OLD.

DON'T WORRY, MOM, WE'RE BIG NOW, WE CAN HELP!

I'LL FIND SOMEWHERE TO WORK!

AND WE HAVE GOOD NEIGHBORS; WE CAN COUNT ON THEM!

YES, I CAN WATCH THE COWS AND I CAN KNIT TOO!

I'LL PRAY WITH YOU. YOU'VE ALWAYS TOLD ME THAT THE GOOD GOD WOULD NEVER ABANDON US!

YES, DEAR, THAT'S TRUE... CAN YOU SAY A PRAYER RIGHT NOW?

DURING THIS PERIOD OF PERSECUTION THE PRACTICE OF RELIGION IS FORBIDDEN, BUT JEANNE LEARNS ABOUT THE CHRISTIAN FAITH FROM HER MOTHER.

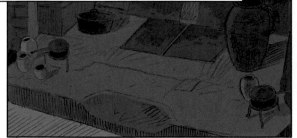

FOR SEVEN YEARS THEY HOPE THAT THEIR FATHER HAS BEEN TAKEN PRISONER BY THE ENGLISH AND IS STILL ALIVE. HOWEVER, EVENTUALLY IT BECOMES CLEAR THAT HE ISN'T COMING BACK.

AT THE AGE OF FIFTEEN, SHE FOUND WORK ABOUT FIVE KILOMETERS FROM HERE.

ARE WE GOING TO GO THERE?

SURE, OFF WE GO TO SAINT COULOMB!

IT IS IN THIS PERIOD THAT JEANNE MAKES A BIG DECISION.

SO YOU'RE NOT GOING TO MARRY THAT NICE SAILOR?

NO, MOTHER.

GOD WANTS ME FOR HIMSELF. HE IS KEEPING ME FOR A WORK AS YET UNKNOWN, FOR A WORK THAT HAS NOT YET BEEN FOUNDED!

YOU SEE, MOTHER, WHEN I WAS SMALL, I LEARNED RIGHT HERE THAT THE POOR COULD HELP EACH OTHER...

LIVING AT THE VISCOUNTESS' HOUSE, I LEARNED THAT THE RICH CAN DO THE SAME... THAT'S WHAT CHARITY IS.

I THINK THAT I'M MEANT TO DEVOTE MYSELF TO THE SERVICE OF THE POOR...

I'M GOING TO LEAVE CANCALE AND TAKE A JOB IN SAINT SERVAN, AT THE HOSPITAL OF THE ROSAIS.

I'M ONLY GOING TO KEEP WHAT I REALLY NEED; THESE ARE MY NICEST CLOTHES, I'M GOING TO GIVE THEM TO MARIE-JOSEPH AND THERESE-CHARLOTTE.

WHY DID SHE GIVE ALL HER CLOTHES TO HER SISTERS?

SHE HAD DECIDED TO DEVOTE HERSELF TO THE SERVICE OF THE POOR; I THINK SHE WANTED TO LOOK AS MUCH LIKE THEM AS POSSIBLE...

WHERE ARE WE GOING NOW, AUNT MARY?

WE'RE GOING TO SAINT SERVAN; THIS WAS AN IMPORTANT STAGE IN JEANNE'S LIFE.

WHY?

YOU'LL SEE AS SOON AS WE GET THERE... WE'RE ALMOST THERE!

AT SAINT SERVAN THE HOSPITAL IS RUN BY WOMEN RELIGIOUS, THE DAUGHTERS OF DIVINE WISDOM.

HELLO... JEANNE JUGAN... WELCOME TO THE ROSAIS, MY CHILD! COME WITH ME!

JEANNE,
WHAT'S THE MATTER?

THIS SPELL ISN'T SURPRISING
AT ALL, YOU POOR THING!
YOU'RE EXHAUSTED!

YOU CAN'T REST HERE,
IT'S NOT GOOD FOR
YOUR HEALTH.
YOU REALLY MUST
GET SOME REST!

TAKE THIS MEDICINE;
YOU'LL FEEL BETTER
RIGHT AWAY.

THANKS, AUNT MARY.

WHAT DID JEANNE DO, AFTER SHE WAS SENT AWAY FROM THE HOSPITAL?

SHE WASN'T SENT AWAY, THOMAS! SHE WAS EXHAUSTED AND SHE REALLY NEEDED TO TAKE CARE OF HERSELF SO THAT SHE COULD RECOVER HER HEALTH!

OH, SO SHE WAS ON SICK LEAVE?

YOU COULD SAY THAT I GUESS, EXCEPT SICK LEAVE DIDN'T EXIST BACK THEN; SHE HAD TO SUPPORT HERSELF.

SO WE SEE JEANNE AT THE END OF HER STRENGTH AFTER SIX YEARS AT THE HOSPITAL OF THE ROSAIS.

SHE THEN FINDS A JOB IN THE HOME OF A VERY NICE OLDER WOMEN WHO ALSO BELONGED TO THE THIRD ORDER, MISS MARIE LECOQ.

OUCH! BLESSED BE GOD!

YOU BURNED YOURSELF AGAIN!

YES.

LEAVE THAT FOR THE MOMENT. WE NEED TO GET READY TO VISIT POOR CONSTANCE; SHE IS SO SICK.

TIME GOES BY. JEANNE RECOVERS. TWELVE YEARS LATER MISS LECOQ FALLS ILL AND JEANNE CARES FOR HER.

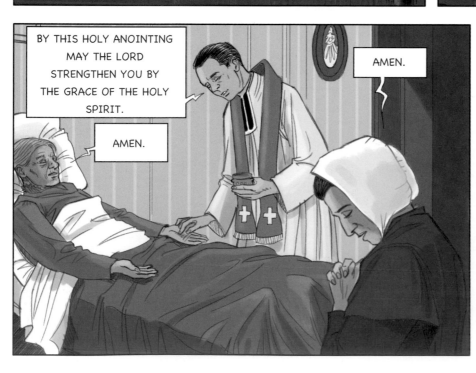

BY THIS HOLY ANOINTING MAY THE LORD STRENGTHEN YOU BY THE GRACE OF THE HOLY SPIRIT.

AMEN.

AMEN.

WE SALUTE YOU, MOST HOLY HEART OF JESUS AND MARY; WE OFFER YOU OUR HEART, RECEIVE IT, POSSESS IT ENTIRELY.

AFTER MISS LECOQ'S DEATH, JEANNE INHERITS A BIT OF MONEY AND SPENDS HER DAYS WORKING FOR WEALTHY FAMILIES IN THE AREA: HOUSEWORK, LAUNDRY, CARING FOR THE SICK...

MUCH LATER, MEMBERS OF THESE FAMILIES WILL BE FOUND AMONG THE LITTLE SISTERS' FIRST BENEFACTORS!

THIS IS THE RUE DU CENTRE. THIS IS WHERE JEANNE RENTED TWO ROOMS WITH A FRIEND OF HERS, FRANCOISE AUBERT, NICKNAMED "FANCHON" AGED 71. NOW, THIS APARTMENT IS CALLED THE "MANSARDE".

A LITTLE WHILE LATER, A 17 YEAR OLD ORPHAN, VIRGINIE TREDANIEL, JOINS THEM.

WINTER 1839.

I'M HAPPY THAT YOU AGREE WITH ME.

WE'RE GOING TO TAKE IN AN ELDERLY WOMAN NAMED ANNE CHAUVIN... SHE CAN SLEEP IN MY BED, THAT WILL BE MORE COMFORTABLE FOR HER.

AND YOU, WHERE ARE YOU GOING TO SLEEP?

IN THE ATTIC, COME SEE! YOU CAN'T IMAGINE ANNE, AT HER AGE, CLIMBING UP THERE, CAN YOU?

I'LL LEAVE YOU TO SLEEP UP THERE ALONE, BECAUSE AT MY AGE I CAN'T IMAGINE CLIMBING UP THERE EITHER!

LOOK, VIRGINIE, A MATTRESS IN THE CORNER, THAT'S ALL I NEED!

JUST A FEW MORE STEPS AND WE'LL BE THERE, ANNE!

SHORTLY AFTER THAT, A SECOND OLD WOMAN,
ISABELLE COEURU, ARRIVED.
THEY WELCOMED HER AND VIRGINIE GAVE HER
HER BED AND WENT TO SLEEP WITH JEANNE
IN THE ATTIC.

AT THIS POINT JEANNE
WAS 47 YEARS OLD.
THIS IS THE REAL
BEGINNING OF HER WORK.
THAT'S WHY WE SAY THAT
SAINT SERVAN WAS SO
IMPORTANT IN HER LIFE.

MARIE JAMET, A FRIEND OF VIRGINIE,
SOON COMES TO HELP THEM. SHE STILL
LIVES WITH HER PARENTS, BUT COMES TO
HELP IN THE EVENING AND ON WEEKENDS.
ViRGINIE AND MARIE HAVE THE SAME
CONFESSOR, FATHER AUGUSTE LE PAILLEUR.

ON OCTOBER 15, 1840,
FATHER LE PAILLEUR
WILL PRESIDE OVER HIS FIRST
MEETING WITH THE WOMEN AT
THE MANSARDE.

NOW WE ARE A REAL CHARITABLE ASSOCIATION.

LET'S PUT IN WRITING THE WAY OF LIFE WE ENVISION FOR OUR MEMBERS...

GOOD IDEA!

TWO MONTHS LATER, MADELEINE BOURGES, A 27 YEAR OLD LAUNDRESS, ARRIVES...

SHE IS SO SICK SHE IS CONVINCED SHE IS DYING AND LEAVES HER FEW POSSESSIONS TO JEANNE'S POOR.

SHE IS WELCOMED AT THE MANSARDE AND CARED FOR SO WELL THAT SHE RECOVERS! SHE THEN JOINS THE GROUP.

GOD GAVE ME BACK MY LIFE; I WANT TO CONSECRATE IT TO HIM!

IT WAS NECESSARY TO FIND A LARGER PLACE TO LIVE.

THESE STAIRS ARE NOT AT ALL PRACTICAL FOR THE ELDERLY.

IN 1841, ALONG WITH THE ELDERLY THEY HAD ALREADY TAKEN IN, JEANNE AND HER COMPANIONS LEFT THE RUE DU CENTRE AND MOVED TO THE RUE DE LA FONTAINE.

WE CAN EASILY FIT TWELVE BEDS HERE!

BUT JEANNE, HOW WILL WE PROVIDE FOR THEM?

THE OLD PEOPLE WERE BEGGARS, WE COULD GO OUT BEGGING IN THEIR PLACE.

THIS IS WHAT JEANNE DOES; SHE IS WELL RECEIVED, BUT HESITATES TO GIVE UP ALL PAID WORK.

SOON AFTER THAT SHE RECEIVES A VISTOR...

HELLO, MADAM, I AM BROTHER CLAUDE-MARIE GANDET AND I BEG FOR THE HOSPITAL OF SAINT JOHN OF GOD IN DINAN...

I'M SORRY... EMBARRASSED REALLY... WE HAVE JUST MOVED HERE WITH SEVERAL ELDERLY PERSONS WE HAVE TAKEN IN AND WE'RE HAVING A HARD TIME MAKING ENDS MEET.

I UNDERSTAND, BUT WHAT DO YOU LIVE ON?

THE GENEROSITY OF A FEW FRIENDS AND SOME BENEFACTORS OF THE ELDERLY WHO HAVE COME TO LIVE WITH US.

JEANNE WILL OFTEN ENCOUNTER FATHER FÉLIX MASSOT. IT IS HE WHO WILL HELP THE LITTLE GROUP MAKE PROGRESS TOWARD LIVING A TRUE RELIGIOUS LIFE AT THE SERVICE OF THE POOR.

AND SO SHE TOOK UP THE PRACTICE OF THE BEGGING, ASKING FOR MONEY, AS WELL AS GIFTS IN KIND… LEFTOVERS OF FOOD, NEEDED CLOTHING AND OTHER MATERIALS.

JEANNE ACCEPTED ALL THAT WAS GIVEN HER. LATER, SHE WILL COUNSEL THE NOVICES TO NEVER THROW ANYTHING AWAY WITHOUT FIRST TRYING TO FIND SOME USE FOR IT.

BUT YOU KNOW, THE BEGGING IS NOT ALWAYS EASY!

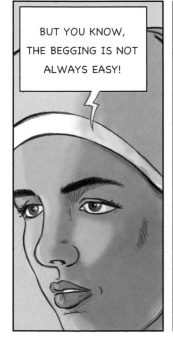

THE SLAP WAS FOR ME. NOW PLEASE GIVE ME SOMETHING FOR MY POOR.

SHE GOT SLAPPED?

THINGS LIKE THAT HAPPENED, BUT LUCKILY IT WASN'T THE GENERAL RULE.

JEANNE, WHAT SHOULD WE CALL YOU NOW?

THE HUMBLE SERVANT OF THE POOR.

COME HERE, THEN, HUMBLE SERVANT OF THE POOR, I HAVE SOME VEGETABLES WAITING FOR YOU!

WHAT? YOU'RE BACK HERE AGAIN? BUT I JUST GAVE YOU SOMETHING YESTERDAY!

THAT IS TRUE, SIR, AND I THANK YOU. BUT MY POOR WERE HUNGRY YESTERDAY, AND THEY ARE HUNGRY AGAIN TODAY.

HM… YES, OF COURSE… WAIT, HERE IS SOMETHING FOR TODAY, AND SINCE YOUR POOR WILL BE HUNGRY AGAIN TOMORROW, DO COME BACK WHENEVER YOU NEED SOMETHING!

THERE REALLY ARE GOOD PEOPLE OUT THERE.

YES, AND IT'S THE SAME WAY TODAY.

LIKE THAT? IS THAT WHAT YOU STILL DO?

YES, OF COURSE! JUST LIKE IN THE BEGINNING, WE PLACE OUR CONFIDENCE IN PROVIDENCE AND WE STILL GO OUT BEGGING TODAY!

WOW!... AND THEN WHAT HAPPENED, AUNT MARY?

HM... ON MAY 29, 1842, THE LITTLE COMMUNITY ELECTED JEANNE AS SUPERIOR AND CHOSE THE NAME, "SERVANTS OF THE POOR."

THEY LIVE POORLY AND JOYFULLY, BUT THEY ARE NOT ALWAYS UNDERSTOOD BY THEIR NEIGHBORS.

WHAT A SCENE! THEY DON'T EVEN HAVE ENOUGH MONEY TO PAY FOR A SEAT IN CHURCH!

ON SEPTEMBER 27, 1842, BISHOP BROSSAIS SAINT-MARC VISITS THE LITTLE COMMUNITY.

I AM VERY HAPPY WITH WHAT I SEE. MAY GOD BLESS YOUR WORK!

WHAT WONDERFUL ENCOURAGEMENT, DON'T YOU THINK, SISTER JEANNE?

YES, WE HAVE TO CONTINUE AND TAKE IN EVEN MORE OF THE POOR!

ON DECEMBER 8, 1843, JEANNE WAS UNANIMOUSLY ELECTED SUPERIOR, BUT ON DECEMBER 23, FATHER LE PAILLEUR GATHERS THE LITTLE COMMUNITY TOGETHER AND NAMES MARIE JAMET SUPERIOR. SHE IS ONLY 23 YEARS OLD!

THAT'S WEIRD, WHY WOULD HE DO THAT?

JEANNE SAID NOTHING. SHE WAS ONLY GOD'S INSTRUMENT. IT WAS HE WHO WAS RESPONSIBLE FOR EVERYTHING.

AND THE OTHERS, THEY DIDN'T SAY ANYTHING?

OUTSIDE THE HOUSE NO ONE KNEW. EVERYONE THOUGHT THAT JEANNE WAS STILL RESPONSIBLE FOR THE HOME.

ON FEBRUARY 4, 1844, THE FIRST FOUR SISTERS TAKE RELIGIOUS NAMES.

JEANNE, WHAT NAME HAVE YOU CHOSEN?

SISTER MARY OF THE CROSS.

SINCE THE BROTHERS OF ST. JOHN OF GOD MAKE THE VOW OF HOSPITALITY, FATHER MASSOT HAS ENCOURAGED US TO ADD IT TO THE OTHER THREE RELIGIOUS VOWS...

DECEMBER 8, 1944.

WE PROMISE GOD TO OBSERVE THE VOWS OF POVERTY, CHASTITY, OBEDIENCE AND HOSPITALITY FOR ONE YEAR.

IN 1845 JEANNE WINS THE MONTYON PRIZE, AN AWARD GIVEN BY THE FRENCH ACADEMY TO "A POOR FRENCH MAN OR WOMAN FOR OUTSTANDINGLY MERITORIUS ACTIVITY." THE PRIZE IS WORTH THREE THOUSAND FRANCS, A FORTUNE AT THAT TIME, AND A GOLD MEDAL.

GREAT FRENCHMEN LIKE CHATEAUBRIAND, LAMARTINE AND VICTOR HUGO BELONGED TO THE FRENCH ACADEMY...

THERE ARE NO WORDS TO DESCRIBE THE ZEAL OF THIS POOR WOMAN WHO GATHERS IN THE POOR! SOMETIMES, WHEN THEY CAN'T WALK, SHE TAKES THEM IN HER ARMS LIKE A PRECIOUS BURDEN, HAPPILY CARRYING THEM HOME.

AH! MR. MAYOR! I'M NOT VERY HAPPY THAT EVERYONE IS TALKING SO MUCH ABOUT ME, BUT THIS PRIZE MONEY HAS ARRIVED JUST IN TIME TO PAY FOR THE ROOF AND THE FURNISHINGS FOR THE NEW BUILDING! WE CAN HAVE THE MEDAL MELTED DOWN TO MAKE A CHALICE FOR THE CHAPEL!

AND THIS "ACADEMY BROCHURE" WILL BE VERY HELPFUL WHEN I GO BEGGING IN OTHER TOWNS!

ARMED WITH THIS BROCHURE JEANNE LEAVES TO BEGIN BEGGING IN RENNES, WHERE SHE WILL SOON ESTABLISH A NEW HOME.

WE'RE GOING TO GO THERE, BUT ON THE WAY WE'RE GOING TO PASS THROUGH DINAN.

YOU SEE, ALL THAT REMAINS IS THE BASE OF THE OLD TOWER WHERE JEANNE STAYED WITH THE FIRST OLD WOMEN IN DINAN. IT WAS AN OLD PRISON, NOT A VERY HEALTHY PLACE TO LIVE.

JEANNE'S REPUTATION BEGAN TO EXTEND BEYOND THE BORDERS OF FRANCE...

WONDERFUL! GREAT JOB! YOU HAVE TO COME TO ENGLAND, SISTER!

IF GOD WILLS IT, I WILL COME!

THE HOUSE OF TOURS IS FOUNDED IN 1847. THEN COMES NANTES, WHERE PEOPLE BEGAN TO CALL US "LITTLE SISTERS OF THE POOR;" THEN PARIS, BESANCON, ETC. OTHER SISTERS ESTABLISH THESE HOUSES. JEANNE GOES TO ANGERS IN 1850...

THERE IS A GOOD STORY ABOUT SAINT JOSEPH ASSOCIATED WITH THIS HOUSE...

FOR THE NEXT TEN YEARS, JEANNE COVERS HUNDREDS OF KILOMETERS IN HER BEGGING ROUNDS, MOSTLY ON FOOT...

AND THEN IN 1852 HER LIFE TAKES ANOTHER TURN.

FATHER LE PAILLEUR SENDS JEANNE TO RENNES, WHICH AT THIS POINT IS THE SITE OF THE MOTHER HOUSE AND NOVITIATE. SHE IS ASKED TO CEASE HER BEGGING ROUNDS, AND EVERYONE IS TOLD NO LONGER TO SPEAK OF HER AS THE FOUNDRESS.

WHILE MARIE AND VIRGINIE MAKE THEIR PERPETUAL PROFESSION IN RENNES IN 1852. JEANNE IS ONLY ALLOWED TO DO SO TWO YEARS LATER.

300 ELDERLY AND 150 LITTLE SISTERS SETTLE INTO THE HOME IN RENNES IN 1855. THERE ARE ALREADY 36 HOUSES, YOUNG WOMEN ARE JOINING THE COMMUNITY IN GREAT NUMBERS AND THE NOVITIATE IS ALREADY TOO SMALL.

WE HAVE A LARGE PROPERTY NEXT TO BECHEREL IN MIND, THE MANOR HOUSE OF LA TOUR.

LA TOUR SAINT JOSEPH WILL BE A CONSTRUCTION SITE FOR OVER TWENTY YEARS.

SENT TO LIVE AMONG THE NOVICES AND POSTULANTS, JEANNE WILL SHARE HER LIFE WITH THEM UNTIL HER DEATH.

DO YOU SEE THE BUILDERS CUTTING THE WHITE STONE FOR THE CHAPEL, HOW BEAUTIFUL THEY MAKE THE STONE?

YES, MY GOOD LITTLE SISTER.

WELL, YOU HAVE TO ALLOW YOURSELF TO BE FORMED LIKE THAT BY OUR LORD.

YOU'VE JUST HEARD ABOUT THE NECESSITY OF DOING PENANCE...

WHAT DOES THIS MEAN? HOW CAN WE DO PENANCE?

FOR EXAMPLE, TWO LITTLE SISTERS GO OUT BEGGING AND THEY ARE LADEN DOWN. IT'S RAINING AND WINDY; THEY'RE SOAKED...

IF THEY ACCEPT THESE INCONVENIENCES GENEROUSLY, SUBMITTING THEMSELVES TO THE WILL OF GOD, THEY ARE DOING PENANCE!

OUR HAPPINESS IS TO BE A LITTLE SISTER OF THE POOR...

IT'S IMPORTANT TO UNDERSTAND THE SIGNIFICANCE OF EACH OF THESE THREE WORDS.

MAKING THE POOR HAPPY, THAT IS EVERYTHING. WE MUST NEVER MAKE THE ELDERLY POOR UNHAPPY.

WE SHOULD SPOIL THEM AS MUCH AS POSSIBLE!

JEANNE OFTEN TOLD THE YOUNG SISTERS, "KNOCK, KNOCK AT THE GATE OF HEAVEN FOR SOULS."

SHE OFTEN SPOKE OF THE HOLY PRESENCE OF GOD IN ONESELF, IN THE TABERNACLE AND IN THE POOR.

SHE TOLD THEM TO LOVE THE POOR VERY MUCH AND TO SEE THEM AS THE SUFFERING MEMBERS OF OUR LORD.

WHATEVER THE CIRCUMSTANCES, IN GOOD TIMES AND BAD, SHE ALWAYS SAID, BLESSED BE GOD! WE MUST ALWAYS SAY, BLESSED BE GOD!...

... GLORY BE TO GOD. ALL FOR HIM. DO EVERYTHING THROUGH LOVE. REFUSE GOD NOTHING!

JESUS IS WAITING FOR YOU IN THE CHAPEL. GO AND FIND HIM WHEN YOU FEEL ALONE AND POWERLESS. TELL HIM "YOU KNOW ALL THAT IS HAPPENING, MY GOOD JESUS. I HAVE ONLY YOU. COME TO MY AID..." AND THEN GO YOUR WAY...

IN THE FOLLOWING YEARS THE NUMBER OF LITTLE SISTERS GROWS QUICKLY.

FATHER LELIÈVRE GIVES HIMSELF WITHOUT COUNTING THE COST, SUPPORTING THE GROWING NUMBER OF FOUNDATIONS.

ENGLAND, BELGIUM, SCOTLAND...

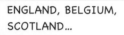

IRELAND, THE UNITED STATES, SPAIN...

ALGERIA, ITALY, MALTA...

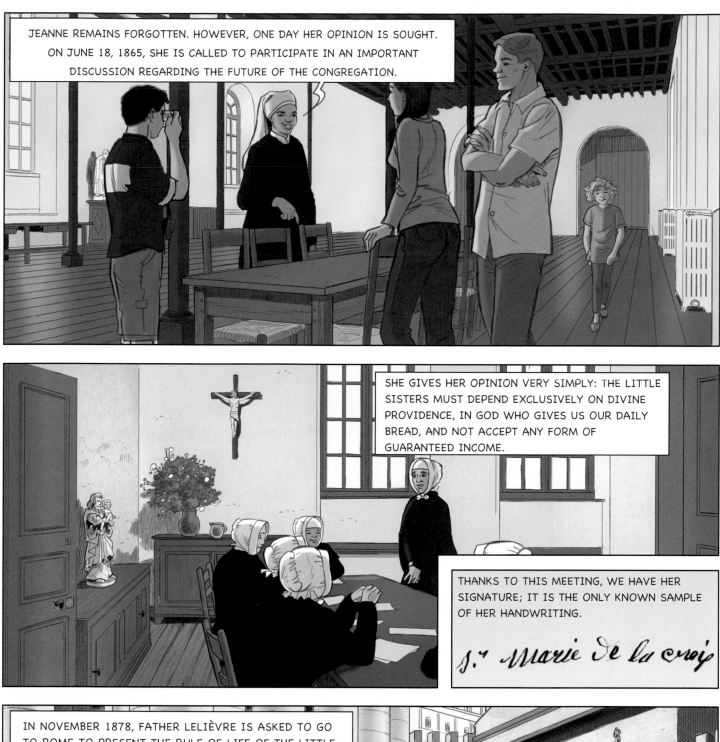

JEANNE REMAINS FORGOTTEN. HOWEVER, ONE DAY HER OPINION IS SOUGHT. ON JUNE 18, 1865, SHE IS CALLED TO PARTICIPATE IN AN IMPORTANT DISCUSSION REGARDING THE FUTURE OF THE CONGREGATION.

SHE GIVES HER OPINION VERY SIMPLY: THE LITTLE SISTERS MUST DEPEND EXCLUSIVELY ON DIVINE PROVIDENCE, IN GOD WHO GIVES US OUR DAILY BREAD, AND NOT ACCEPT ANY FORM OF GUARANTEED INCOME.

THANKS TO THIS MEETING, WE HAVE HER SIGNATURE; IT IS THE ONLY KNOWN SAMPLE OF HER HANDWRITING.

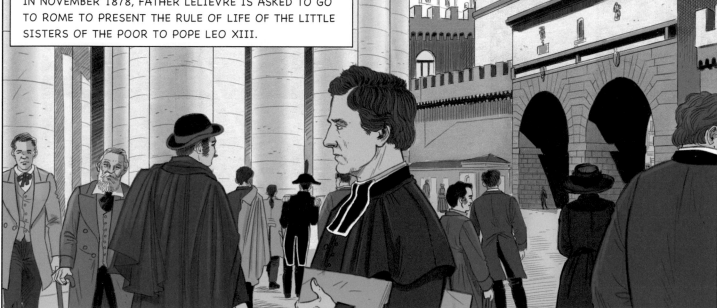

IN NOVEMBER 1878, FATHER LELIÈVRE IS ASKED TO GO TO ROME TO PRESENT THE RULE OF LIFE OF THE LITTLE SISTERS OF THE POOR TO POPE LEO XIII.

41

"ETERNAL FATHER, OPEN YOUR GATES TODAY TO THE MOST MISERABLE OF YOUR CHILDREN, BUT ONE WHO GREATLY LONGS TO SEE YOU ... O MARY, MY DEAR MOTHER, COME TO ME. YOU KNOW THAT I LOVE YOU AND THAT I LONG TO SEE YOU."
THE LAST WORDS OF SISTER MARY OF THE CROSS.

AND THEN?

AND THEN, ON AUGUST 29, 1879, JEANNE DIES. SHE WAS 86 YEARS OLD. SHE IS BURIED WITHOUT ANY SPECIAL RECOGNITION.

SHE DIED FORGOTTEN...

BUT TODAY, MANY PEOPLE COME TO THE CRYPT TO PRAY AT HER TOMB.

WHAT DO THOSE DATES MEAN?

1792 JEANNE JUGAN 1879

BEATIFIEE le 3 Oct. 1982

CANONISEE le 11 Oct. 2009

OCTOBER 11, 2009. ROME.

I WAS THERE! IT WAS AWESOME TO HEAR POPE BENEDICT XVI PROCLAIM HER A "SAINT" SAYING,

"JEANNE JUGAN WAS CONCERNED WITH THE DIGNITY OF HER BROTHERS AND SISTERS IN HUMANITY WHOM AGE HAD MADE VULNERABLE, RECOGNIZING IN THEM THE PERSON OF CHRIST HIMSELF."

OH! OUR JEANNE JUGAN, A SAINT!

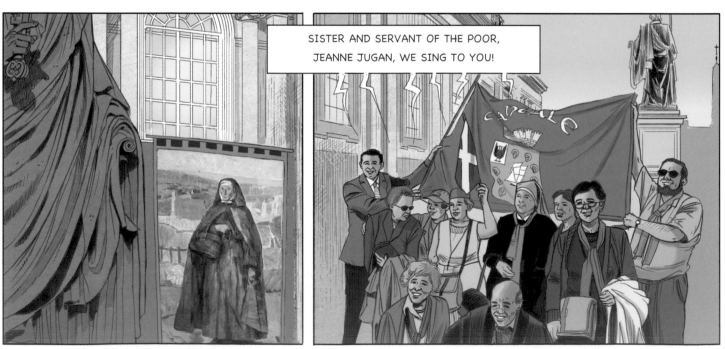

SISTER AND SERVANT OF THE POOR, JEANNE JUGAN, WE SING TO YOU!

CLAIRE WE'RE MOVING ON, ARE YOU COMING?

GOOD AFTERNOON!

BUENAS TARDES!

BONJOUR!

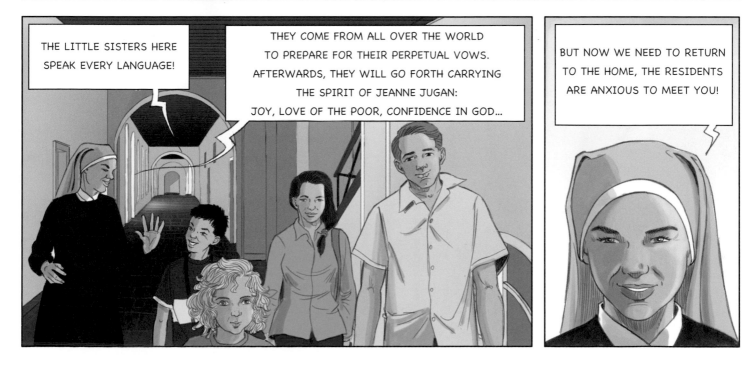

THE LITTLE SISTERS HERE SPEAK EVERY LANGUAGE!

THEY COME FROM ALL OVER THE WORLD TO PREPARE FOR THEIR PERPETUAL VOWS. AFTERWARDS, THEY WILL GO FORTH CARRYING THE SPIRIT OF JEANNE JUGAN: JOY, LOVE OF THE POOR, CONFIDENCE IN GOD...

BUT NOW WE NEED TO RETURN TO THE HOME, THE RESIDENTS ARE ANXIOUS TO MEET YOU!

YOU KNOW, WHEN I WAS YOUR AGE, I COULD RUN THAT FAST!

YOU KNOW, AUNT MARY, I THINK I UNDERSTAND. SAINT JEANNE JUGAN ISN'T DEAD! EVERYTHING SHE DID GOES ON TODAY! SHE IS STILL ALIVE!

DIDIER CHARDEZ 2012

After reading about Saint Jeanne Jugan for the first time, people often want to learn more.

Jeanne Jugan lives on today on five continents.

We invite you to visit the website:

www.littlesistersofthepoor.org (USA)
www.littlesistersofthepoor.ie (Ireland & UK)
www.littlesistersofthepoor.org.au (Oceania)
www.lsptw.org (Taiwan)

Jesus, you rejoiced and praised your Father
for having revealed to little ones
the mysteries of the Kingdom of Heaven.
We thank you for the graces granted
to your humble servant, Jeanne Jugan,
to whom we confide our petitions and needs.

Father of the Poor,
you have never refused the prayer of the lowly.
We ask you, therefore, to hear the petitions
that she presents to you on our behalf.

Jesus, through Mary, your Mother and ours,
we ask this of you, who live and reign
with the Father and the Holy Spirit now and forever.
Amen.